DOG LANGUAGE

BY CHASE TWICHELL

COPPER CANYON PRESS

Printed in the United States of America

Cover art: Joel Adas, *Garden Games* (detail), 1993. Oil on canvas, 66 x 84 inches. Copyright 1993 by Joel Adas.

Copper Canyon Press is in residence at Fort Worden State Park in Port Townsend, Washington, under the auspices of Centrum Foundation. Centrum is a gathering place for artists and creative thinkers from around the world, students of all ages and backgrounds, and audiences seeking extraordinary cultural enrichment.

LIBRARY OF CONGRESS CATALOGING-IN-PUBLICATION DATA
Twitchell, Chase, 1950–
Dog language / Chase Twitchell.
    p. cm.
ISBN 1–55659–231–0 (pbk. : alk. paper)
    I. Title
PS3570.W47D64 2005
811'.54—DC22

                                    2005008865

98765432
FIRST PRINTING

COPPER CANYON PRESS
Post Office Box 271
Port Townsend, Washington 98368
www.coppercanyonpress.org

To my sisters, Eliza and Cary,

and in memory of my father
Charles Pratt Twichell
1924–2004

ACKNOWLEDGMENTS

America Zen: A Gathering of Poets, ed. Larry Smith and Ray MacNiece (Bottom Dog, 2004): "The All of It," "Next and Last," "The Quality of Striving," "Rain in Ivy," "Soul in Space"

Blackbird: "Dangerous Playgrounds," "Joyride"

The Georgia Review: "Cocktail Music," "Death's Portrait," "Dog Biscuits," "A Negative of Snow," "Tech Help"

Hayden's Ferry Review: "Crèche"

Hotel Amerika: "Cities of Mind," "Vestibule"

Indiana Review: "The Art of the Kiss"

The Iowa Review: "A Lamb by Its Ma," "No One's Mother"

Kenyon Review: "Centaur," "Dream Baby," "Infant Pearls"

Lake Effect: "The Tail"

Lasting: Poetic Visions of Aging (Pima Press, 2005): "The Ceiling," "The Range," "Verizon"

Ontario Review: "The Ceiling," "Fake Polio," "Neck Exercises," "Verizon"

Ploughshares: "My Listener," "New England Slate Pane"

Poetry: "Animal Caution," "Self-portrait"

Salmagundi: "Arcade," "Skeleton," "Tutelage"

Shade: "The Fork in the Moment," "Sorry," "What the Grownups Are Saying"

Slate: "Sling"

Tin House: "Cinderblock"

Urthona: "Marijuana," "Next and Last"

The Wisdom Anthology of North American Buddhist Poetry, ed. Andrew Schelling (Wisdom Publications, 2005): "Let's Talk," "Marijuana," "My Listener," "The Paper River," "The Quality of Striving," "Topiary Rooster," "Tutelage"

The Yale Review: "Auld Lang Syne," "Marijuana," "The Paper River," "Topiary Rooster"; recipients of the Smart Family Foundation Award, 2004.

"No One's Mother" and "A Lamb by Its Ma" are dedicated to Mary Eliott Clark Wilson. "The Wheelchair in the Attic" is for my cousin Sam Clement, my childhood's true friend. Sam speaks for himself in the poem. "The Fork in the Moment" belongs to Sarah Hartshorne, "Mah-jongg" to Lucy Kasofsky, "The Pack" to Andrus Nichols, and "Infant Pearls" to Sharon Olds. "Monastery Nights" is dedicated to Sam Hamill, and "Work Libido" to Hayden Carruth. Deep gratitude to Charlie Williams. Always Russell.

Hi, Mom!

CONTENTS

1. SUNDAY NOON

2. ICICLE

3. LASER SAFARI

1. SUNDAY NOON

SKELETON

No one dead will ever
read these words,
and those alive now
will sweep them from the streets.
The writing of our time most
likely to survive is graffiti.
It survives war.
So why not spray letters
you can see a long way off,
"the plain picture,"
as Bob Dylan put it.
"Truth. . . ," he said. "Why,
truth is just the plain picture."

The dogs run through half-thawed
woods, barking the holy scary
words rote in a child,
ruins and crosses and bones,
never outgrown.
And they dig at the gray roses
of hives collapsed in snow,
nothing but paper, words
saying there was honey once.

I asked Truth what to worship,
and Truth said Death,
looking up from licking
the caviar of moments
from Death's hand.
So here are the bones
in the exploded view,
pelvis and vertebrae,
thrown dice of hands.
Look at the skull.
I'm its voice.

THE PAPER RIVER

The most beloved body
of my childhood was Johns Brook,
its bed of ancient broken pears,
icy libations pouring
over them for centuries.
Through the leaky oval mask
I entered its alcoves and grand halls,
its precincts of green-brown light,
the light of my infant thinking.
In the minnow-bright roar
I saw the place where life and art
meet under water, stone to stone,
with the sunken treasure and trash.
The sound of the brook
was the sound of the house,
the pools of the kitchen and bedrooms.
A galaxy away it would still be
the background of my sleep.

Clouds came down to earth,
great gloomy rooms among the trees,
dark rooms of the brook,
church of deep pools.
As soon as you entered
you were wholly alone in it,
all sinewy ladders
and gray stairs, stones magnified,
and the sidelong trout,
all gone now,
rainbows and brookies,
one big one per pool,
gills like fresh cuts.

I dove into the flume's mystery,
no place you could touch bottom
or see all the way down in
because half at least
was always in shadow.
It was like learning a room
by carrying a candle
corner to corner,
looking for God to see if He too
was awake and listening
to the river crumpling and erasing,
enforcing its laws.
I found a cold, an oblique god
who commanded me to answer
all my questions by myself.

The English language
is also a beautiful river,
full of driftwood and detritus,
bones hung with trinkets,
scant beaches more stones than sand.
And up on the hills it's the wind
touching the juniper spurned
by the cows, its thistle sharpness,
and the fawn's hoof
left by coyotes,
in their scat.

DANGEROUS PLAYGROUNDS

The father is teaching his eight-year-old
to clean a grouse, the purple-gray skin
pimpled by plucking,
and so delicate that one roughly pulled
pinch of feathers could tear it,
with little bruises where
the shot went in.
If you push on the bumpy
sole of a foot, the toes
wrap around your finger
like a baby's hand. It's a reflex.
He says *clean*, not *gut*
as the other fathers do,
the organs slippery and ruby,
nothing soft, even the liver
rubbery, and the heart
hard as an unripe cherry,
all of it smelling
like neither excrement nor sex,
but something in between.

At the piano someone's great-uncle
entertained the children in the uninsulated
octagonal room, clean Yankee architecture
a century old. We sang "Auld Lang Syne"
and *I have ridden the wind,*
I have ridden the sea,
I have ridden the ghosts that flee
from the vaults of death
with a chilling breath
over all of Galilee.
I already knew that words
do not live entirely inside language.

No one told me;
I could see exactly where the breaches were,
the place we're supposed to turn around
and go back. Beyond that was the sting,
electric fence, and beyond that
a feather caught in a twig,
strange graft,
and I made a note to myself:
don't ignore this,
thus inviting the sting.

I often think about the doll's house
in *The Tale of Two Bad Mice*
by Beatrix Potter.
While the two dolls were out,
Tom Thumb and his wife-mouse
Hunca Munca briefly set up housekeeping
there, though it was a disappointment—
the miniature plaster foods inedible,
the lead knife bending on the painted ham,
nothing real, nothing as they expected.
In their disillusionment
they vandalized the place,
smashing the lobster glued to its plate,
jamming the fake fish into the fake fire.
It was a scene of seduction and abandonment,
the riches glimmering all around them,
and then the joke.

THE FORK IN THE MOMENT

Sometimes a sentence has to go forth
into the world like an eldest child
and be the first one, the only kid in the class
who knows all about sex
and has to live with the secret knowledge,
knowledge like the first fizz out of the soda bottle.

A car horn was honking and honking
in the woods by the construction site,
maybe somebody calling for help,
its rhythm the only key to its meaning.
It was steady for a while, purposeful,
then let silence and twilight wash over it
for a few minutes, then resumed,
then stopped. I didn't go down there;
I didn't call the police. There was nothing
about it in the paper all week.

Remember Toby Tyler,
the boy who ran off with the circus?
And Huck with his slingshot,
zinging crab apples at cars?
We hid out in the woods
on the near side of adolescence,
barefoot, starting fires with a stick,
never going home.
We had a pact to live outside
the adult world forever,
and we broke it.
I climbed the chain link to get in,
dropping down hard
so that I felt my feet in my jaws.
We lost each other. Nothing was left

of the trees but stumps like gravestones:
Huck Finn, Toby Tyler, and me.

SORRY

I'm to press the pad of my thumb
against the trout's upper jaw,
its teeth surprisingly sharp,
more like berry cane than teeth,
its eyes already beginning to look back
from the afterlife. It's limbless,
like a whole soul in my hands,
and slimy, so I clamp it
with my knees to get a better grip
and use both thumbs
to force back the jaw until the spine
breaks slowly, like a green stick,
and the jaws half close
as if by failing memory.
Then later in the sink we slit
open the belly, strip out the guts,
see if it's male or female,
see what it's eaten. If it's female
Dad clicks *sorry* with his tongue.

CENTAUR

The first typeface I loved
was Centaur, cut by Bruce Rogers
in 1914. It had animal bones
and reminded me
of skinny-dipping at night,
baptized in star water so cold
I suddenly became another
animal from the waist down.

In childhood, I knew
all about the Minotaur,
Cyclops, and centaurs.
My father read to me
about the man-horses,
so I had an inkling
of their danger
and thereafter leaned
toward the horse part
and away from the man.

FAKE POLIO

A dog star, pole star, north star
shone on my native country,
Depression.
We thought you had polio,
said my mother,
which may be why
I wanted braces with tiny rubber bands
like Pauline's,
Toby's crutches and cast.

We lived at the foot of a cul-de-sac,
so home was downhill from the school's
dirt parking lot where we jumped bikes
off logs and boards
and each summer a big mulberry
stained the cement walks.
Oh, to feel those
bike-riding muscles again.

NO ONE'S MOTHER

I aim my mind toward
Ghostland, Afterlife,
wherever she may be,
Mary, tart Scot trained
to raise other people's kids,
to feed and bathe and discipline.
Get crackin'! she'd say,
snapping at our fannies
with a wet dish towel.
Get crackin'!
Get off with ye!

I've got a dozen kinds of mint,
fast-spreading neighborhoods
by the shed. Pang of longing
for Mary, her fingers loosening
the soil around the runners,
menthol shoots.
She liked her first husband
better than the other one.
She threw my plastic flute
over a cliff because it bugged her.
She was no one's mother.
She stayed with us when
our mother was gone.
When my father brought
his girlfriend to the pool,
she told him to beat it
and he obeyed.

A LAMB BY ITS MA

Just before it rains, the lilacs
thrash weakly,
storm light heightening
the clusters drooping
at their peak of scent,
wind running
through them like slow water,
then a splash, mood swing:
leaves spangled with drops
from inside the storm.
Mary made us come inside
if there was lightning,
flapping a white towel
to call us back.
We hung around the kitchen
drinking tea till it cleared.
She brought us tea at bedtime.
A good cup of black tea
and you'll sleep like a lamb by its ma.
She told us that our parents
loved us, that their war
was theirs alone.
She said it in the charged air,
in the scent of their absence
from the house,
their clean absence.
If thunder came at night,
she told about the brave
and faithful dogs of Scotland,
how a shepherd knows
where his lamb has gone
by bits of wool in the wire.

WHAT THE GROWNUPS ARE SAYING

Don't you want to hear
what the grownups are saying?
Let's eavesdrop from the balcony.
Those parties had currents,
an undertow of scent,
low-throttled approvals of male cars
idling through a three-hour dinner
and come-what-may, more drinks later
and the bird laughter pitched slightly high.
Mrs. M always played with the candles.
She'd snap off the weak stalagmites
and feed them back into the fire.
When the wives got drunk
they spilled secrets,
retelling the stories and adding
a few details no one knew,
then getting milked for the rest.
How Mrs. C stole Mr. M's clothes
skinny-dipping in '58
and Mr. M walked into town
with a maple twig, looking for a phone.
The two deer killed with one shot.
The talking ran like a brook through the house
then out into the icy lake of knowledge,
beyond the known words to where the water
began to smell like the sea,
and the first feathers of the undertow
began their inventive caressing.
Tonight we've found a box of Tampax
in Mom's bathroom, and just before dessert
we'll shoot all forty white mice with tails
over the railing into the perfumed clouds below.

I'm not hurting them, her and him.
I'm just keeping them locked
in these pronouns for a while
so I can study them,
almost closing the door on them,
but not quite. They're washing up,
the guests gone home,
and cannot hear that outside
in the background of the world
the voice of the party continues,
its words ascending the stairs
into the child's ear ad infinitum.

WATERTOWN

Watch out for easily broken
crocus and tulip—
lift the spoils from them
carefully, hit the brakes
for chocolates in colored foils,
caramels.
Grandma had a hard sugar egg
you could look inside:
paper ducks, spring flowers,
but the pond was crystalline
midwinter blue.
Also inside the eyehole:
the door to the next room
that you can never enter,
even glimpse.
You'd have to break the room
to break the door.
The scene never aged,
so the mystery lived on
in the pastel bunnies and chicks
even though Grandma took us
to a farm to watch them
candle eggs, and you could see
the chicken embryos
hunched up in there
like little monks.

And yes, there were rooms
of golden light setting off
paint colors Grandpa named
Artichoke, Ember—
green, red, gold.

She wore red, black,
white. Nice painting.

Grandpa's famous cocktail,
the Sunday Noon:
three parts freshly squeezed
orange juice, two parts lemon,
one lime, six parts gin.
Big cold-clouded pitchers,
glasses with sugar on the rim.
Who wants to grow up in a land
of jousting knights and mah-jongg,
God-relics of Africa and old California,
cherries in a chilled silver bowl?
I do, I do.

Grandma had a hundred-year-old
jade tree on the piano.
I'm possessed by a need
to have one exactly like it—
coins of green water,
bark like elephant hide.
Hers had a glazed pot,
a stone turtle.
I want that turtle.

THE WHEELCHAIR IN THE ATTIC

Sam remembers me mimicking
my father at Sunday lunch,
saying whatever he said—
The fish! The fish!—
recalling Florida, 1959,
sniffing as if he can smell it
(the snapper my sister Eliza
tried to cook on a radiator.
We were bored. It was Florida).
He calls for the story and in his wake
I echo *The fish! The fish!*

Lunch was a formal sit-down,
linens and finger bowls,
cousins and siblings conversing
under the radar of adults,
me at Gran's left as usual—
Starvation Corner, served last
by Hilke from Finland.
Afterward, Sam and I would hike
two flights of back stairs,
past a room of blue linoleum
once servants' quarters:
three hospital beds
beneath the northern eaves—
Sam says, *They must've gotten a special
at the TB sanatorium*—
and into the half-empty,
house-sized main room,
its vaulted, uninsulated roof
rising to a single point,
and avenues of boxes
through which we rummaged,

leaving no trace
on the little mummies
of train cars in newspaper,
the clothes of our infant parents.
On shelves, the heads Gran
sculpted in her artistic days looked away
from one another, one of each child,
clay cold and moist
as if recently worked,
but they were old, and their noses
had been pinched shut.
(I didn't do it.)

When I asked Sam about the wheelchair,
he said, *It was chrome with a green seat*
and foot plates that flipped up
for extra traction. It folded up;
I remember trying to ride it narrow-
or normal-width while standing
on the twin pipes between the big rear tires.

Eyes shut, one rode
while the other steered
through shafts of book dust
to the dormers' dead ends,
backing, circling to confuse the rider,
past the locked piano,
cradle of Christmas lights,
each time a different route,
cedar and chimney-damp,
row of zippered bags.
Then the rider guessed where he was.

Under a loose board
we hid a folded paper

in the dingy fluff of insulation.
What did it say?
Sam remembers no such paper,
just jacks, and a crystal filched from a lamp.

Oh Sam, don't you want to glide
back to that peaceful gloom,
navigating by camphor and mouse-smell
the few tight turns,
not talking about the family?
I tried to lose myself,
to not know where I was,
but I always knew.
As for what's under the floor,
Sam suggests we *approach*
the current owners on some pretext or other
then slip up to the attic for a look-see.

What Sam doesn't know
is that when I was sent from the table
for my mimicry,
my father followed me upstairs
and I said it was because
he no longer loved my mother,
and he said, *You're wrong.*
It's your mother who does not love me.

TOPIARY ROOSTER

Five thirty on a summer afternoon,
Mom's sharpening a knife.
Dad comes in like a river current,
a hard little swirl around him
like muscles but of the air.
The first cork's been pulled,
tepee of kindling built in the grill.
Tonight it's about the rooster again,
Mom's topiary beheaded by Dad
because all these years
he thought that end was the tail.
I'm working on the conversion
of my handwriting from yarn
to razor wire, making a list of words
that seem to have inner lives:
marinade, carbon steel.
Eliza's there beside me, staging
a wedding of the pepper to the salt.

Some two-cycle machine starts up
in the valley, bringing back the scream
and smell of burned wood from his saw,
his lathe whining spirals to the floor.
She'd be shut up in their bedroom,
mid-afternoon, hardly any sound,
but the breath said it was weeping.
Did I already have my own
sadness apart from hers?
One that might run together
with a rivulet of hers?
I think so, but she didn't want
to touch sorrows with me.
She lay waiting for some psychic

match to strike her life back to the way
it was supposed to be,
with a closet full of dresses
not yet imagined,
and late sun agleam
on the scotch-colored
hills of Connecticut.

My mind goes up into the high pines
and sits among the crows.
I can hear Harry Belafonte singing
Come back Liza, come back girl,
which always made my sister cry.
How easily that song is put out
by a swish of wind!
Still, I stay up there for a while
above the house as it was then:
painted to match the granite
on which it was built,
with lichen-colored trim,
and two kids watching their mother
sharpen her long-bladed shears
then continue to snip away
at the rooster, lush and fully formed,
the way he should have been.

Don't go back, say the crows.
Stay here in the gold opening
left by the storm, quick storm,
big truck passing on the highway,
gone now behind the washed and dazzling clouds.
Let all the words go.
They come from elsewhere
and long ago, are immigrants here.
They should return to their faraway homes.

They should fly up to city balconies
and preen there,
or land like a big shadow on the cornfield
and pick among the stalks.

CRÈCHE

The December I was thirteen
and Cary two, I'd push her buggy
through the dusk, a few blocks
of shoveled sidewalk to the church,
where a life-size plaster family
had set up camp: Mary,
dull Joseph, their spot-lit doll.
While Jesus hid behind a sleeping cow,
Cary herself would ascend
to the manger, all eyes upon her:
simple shepherds' eyes,
jeweled eyes of kings,
sheep, camel eyes all watching her
climb in her stiff red snowsuit
into the milk crate,
her own eyes clouding
with some pleasure to which
I was already inured.
I wanted to be none of them,
especially not Mary,
who had to give birth
having never known love.

CHAIN SAW

The trunk's roped to fall
back into the woods
and not toward the house.
They take the top first,
dismantling the great ladder,
no limbs cracking,
nothing falling,
but lowered by cables
then chipped and sprayed
back into the woods.
They leave the stump.
Soon ferns will grow there
in the duff.
As far as I know,
cousin Sam was the last
to climb it, in the early sixties—
he'd have been ten or twelve.
He reached the spot my father
did at the same age: strong fork,
last reliable seat, the family seat,
white pine a century old,
the height of the dominion,
staying up there for a while
in medicinal air, overlooking
Gran's roof, the apple trees,
the car, the relatives gathering
in the reddening day,
the hour of nostalgia, the alpenglow.
Sam saw the scar
of his initials, and the date.

COCKTAIL MUSIC

All my life a brook of voices
has run in my ears,
many separate instruments
tuning and playing, tuning.
It's cocktail music,
the sound of my parents
in their thirties,
glass-lined ice bucket loaded
and reloaded but no one tending bar,
little paper napkins, cigarettes,
kids passing hors d'oeuvres.
It's drinking music,
riffle of water over stones,
ice in glasses, rise and fall
of many voices touching—
that music. Husbands grilling meat,
squirting the fire to keep it down,
a joke erupting, bird voices snipping
at something secret by the bar.
It's all the voices collapsed
into one voice,
urgent and muscled like a river
then lowered as in a drought,
but never gone. It's the background.
When I lift the shell to my ear
it's in there.

2. ICICLE

NEUROTRANSMISSION

My history of drug-taking is long,
starting with One-A-Day vitamins
and St. Joseph's aspirin for children;
pills for migraine and insomnia;
marijuana, tea, wine;
and then the Solaces, one by one,
a Noah's ark of creatures too weak
to haul away another's sorrows,
though they lent their weight.
Now a psychopharmacologist
oversees the weather of my brain
and I live in its atmospheres,
its tides, its own distinctive
forms of sentience.

DREAM BABY

What if you could dream
what you dreamed as a baby?
You'd have to abandon
this consciousness
in which we converse
to re-inhabit the mindless
and bodiless infant senses,
the cells of the baby's dream
dividing. Not me:
A bat and a night-light
made scary shadows in my room.
I knocked on the wall
but no one came.

AULD LANG SYNE

Perfume of snow
melting in the hall,
on the slates.
Dull with old smoke,
the eyes of the moose preside;
his antlers uphold
someone's wet gloves.
He has a bald spot on his neck
where people stroke him for luck,
and a wreath of balsam.
At fifteen I touched the place
where the world touched him.
Fly back, wild flocks of the senses,
eavesdrop at the shrines
of the fireplace and bar.
Bring something back:
live coal of lipstick
or some resinous
perfume for the New Year.

Summers, we'd steal out onto
the golf course of the private club
to make love under the Perseid showers,
soaked by the wet velvet green.
They were just boys,
but we longed for them
and lay with them.
Who would refuse such an imprint?
I wear it still like a string of cold beads.

There's a virgin sadness trapped
in the old house, museum of summer,
furnace cranked up for Christmas.

The adults stir their cocktails with icicles.
The kids kiss in the halls.
Four generations of match-strikes
stripe the blackened hearth.
The fire-eyes of the andiron owls
are watching the men, who have
wrapped the dog in a towel.
Mrs. M's bleared mouth
repeats that *quills*
are hydraulic—cut off the tips
and they'll come right out,
which turns out to be untrue.
They use pliers, and afterward
the dog wags in apology
and the drinking resumes.

MARIJUANA

Stoned by noon, I'd take the trail
that runs along the X River
in the State of Y, summer of '69,
crows' black ruckus overhead.
I'd wade through the ferns' sound
of vanishing to the almost-invisible ledge,
stark basin canted out to the southwest:
sheltered, good drainage,
full sun, remote, state land.
You could smell the blacker, foreign green
from a long way off when it rained,
incense-grade floral, the ripening spoils,
then pang of wood smoke,
antiseptic pitch and balsam,
scents cut like initials into a beech,
then cold that kills the world for a while,
puts it under, then wakes it up
again in spring when it's still tired.
I woke from its anesthetic
wanting the tight buds of my loneliness
to swell and split, not die in waiting.
It was why I rushed through everything,
why I tore away at the perpetual gauze
between me and the stinging world,
its starlight and resins,
new muscle married to smoke and tar,
just wedding the world for a while.
About to divorce it, too,
to marry some other smoke and tar.

On snowshoes in falling snow,
we lugged peat, manure,
and greensand a mile up there.

Alfalfa meal, spent hops.
The clones bronzed, hairy and sticky,
and a week before frost we'd slice
the dirt around them with a bread knife,
which gave the dope
a little extra turpentine.
Weed, reefer, smoke—
it was one of life's perfumes.
Sometimes its flower opens
on a city street, gray petals,
phantom musk dispersing.

Sleeping out on the high ledges
on a bed of blueberries dwarfed
by wind and springy beneath the blankets,
we'd watch for meteors and talk till dawn,
gazing toward the pinnacle in the distance,
pyramid to the everlasting glory
of Never Enough, not far below us
in his tomb, asleep in the granite chill
with the bones of his faithful animals.

Could this be the pinnacle?
To be slumming back there,
buoyant on the same old
wave just breaking,
now the wave of words, the liftoff?
I'm still cracking open the robin's egg
to see the yellow heart, the glue.
A pinnacle is a fulcrum,
a scale. And now that it's tipped
I can look back through the ghost
of self-consciousness to its embryo,
first the tomboy,
then the chick in a deerskin skirt,

the first breaking of the spirit,
the heart's deflowerment.

Caw, caw, a crow wants to peck
at the ember of the mind
as it was before it tasted
the dark meat of the world.
But I can call it back—
the match's sulfur spurt,
its petals of carbon and tar,
a flash of mind, a memory:
how after each deflowerment
I became the flower.

THE ALL OF IT

I stood naked in the icy brook
under stars. I lay on hot granite
crisped with pearl-gray lichen
we crushed beneath us.

He tied trout flies with dog hair
and feathers, cooked the little fish
over the coals, on green sticks
he later burned, leaving nothing.

Was that it? Exactly that,
the Inside Knowledge,
the All of it?

THE ART OF THE KISS

Kiss your third and fourth fingers
where they meet the palm.
That's how it feels.
I'd kissed a boy—
that *was* what it was like,
not the stinging adult
kisses of history and salt,
or kisses nipped and inflamed,
chancre-hearted,
with nothing inside
but the dust of the flower,
or the kiss of the little trout
blackening in the fire,
the words it draws like flies,
even now. Pink flesh,
translucent bones.

THE LAST KNOT

Because you are dead,
the last knot is mine to untie,
the last drawer mine
to hold upside down
over the trash.
You were cruel, first love.
The beauty you made
in my eye blinded me
while your body wed me,
so all the years of my youth
I was your widow,
and remain, even now,
though I forget you unforgiven,
one of your widows.

TUTELAGE

Stone ruins of a monastery,
door still standing,
starving horse tied to a tree.
My dog is lost—I call
but no one comes.
I dream this repeatedly.

When the student is ready,
the teacher appears.
And if the student is not?
Is still a child?
Words in a red notebook,
not hymns. I never chose
my teachers or their gods,
peering down together
over the pall of Modern Europe,
algebra's barbed wire,
the barking (in French) of Monsieur.
Heart-to-hearts concerning
discipline and striving.
Heartless tests.
Surrogate family. What a laugh.
Bye-bye, the whole lot of you.

Fair are the meadows,
fairer still the woodlands—
words and woodlands
briefly simultaneous—
maybe *that* was God?
And childhood?
A wind blew through it,
stealing shingles,
breaking branches,

not saying thank you,
not saying good-bye.

I will not speak of my first tutor.
He was my tutor and no one else's.
I dedicate this poem to the flies
that came to the wound.

BONSAI

What's pornographic about them
is the intimacy with which one
can regard the other: the one
made to be displayed—
five berries, red, helpless at the hands,
the fingers and scissors of the other,
while the other can scrutinize
from any angle whenever it wants.
That's the obscenity.

Listen, former self:
you're a child.
I no longer have a child in me.
I feel my bones in the handrail,
tree skeleton, hardwood
that remembers how the human
got into its body,
the tree into the little tree.
I'm no one's mother now.
I abandon you here.
I'll speak of you no more.

SELF-PORTRAIT

I know I promised to stop
talking about her,
but I was talking to myself.
The truth is, she's a child
who stopped growing,
so I've always allowed her
to tag along, and when she brings
her melancholy close to me
I comfort her. Naturally
you're curious; you want to know
how she became a gnarled branch
veiled in diminutive blooms.
But I've told you all I know.
I was sure she had secrets,
but she had no secrets.
I had to tell her mine.

NEXT AND LAST

Eating almonds and drinking
jasmine tea. Each almond
has its own fingerprint of flavor,
and each sip of tea.
I'm unfaithful to both
the moment just passing
and the new one's
infant pain of sprouting,
the swelling gist
breaking the husk.
I'm a bee gathering gold dust,
one of the winged seeds
spiraling through November's
ocher underthings,
a moving target,
reflex, spasm, distraction,
sun behind a cloud—
two moments not even strung,
the passing and the new,
but blown for a nanosecond
by the same wind.

Faraway leaves haunt the tea,
also kid voices barely there and not
for long, so if I want to hear their
last words I have to commit
to hearing them right here, right now.
Or the pot cools
and the ghosts go away forever.

ORPHANAGE

Wolf Jaws, Basin, Noonmark, Big Slide—
I always excise the names of mountains
from the poems. I post that land: KEEP OUT.
My bones are betrothed to it,
and graves are private.

A centaur appeared
in the tomboy's mind,
androgynous creature
more animal than human,
perhaps half girl,
and remains there intact,
so I can study it
up close in perfect safety.

So many fish, in middle age,
and so few caught, just one or two
so small you had to throw them back.

I made a shoebox stable
with scissors, tape, thin cardboard.
It had mangers and half-high
doors that opened and closed,
row of plastic heads looking out.
My parents named me Penelope,
which, combined with Twichell,
invited wordplay. It was hard
for Felicity Tuttle and me.
The coydogs on the hills
still howl the original syllables.
The horses neigh them
in their cardboard stalls.

3. LASER SAFARI

ARCADE

I write for the euphoria
of thunderstorms,
gravity and uplift at once,
and the *jing-jing-jing* of luck
in the arcade's private rooms.
I play here every day
in the maze of thinking,
of music and weeping and visions:
someone cracking ice in the kitchen,
a ghost in a silver chair.
Where else can I
find the half-human girl
with dog blood in her veins,
or crash again at the condemned hotel,
empty after the auction,
in which our pack met and coupled,
talked and smoked pot
until the fire department persuaded
the owners to let them burn it
so the men could practice
on controlled fire?

In Japan, pachinko's everywhere.
What a beautiful toy the boys have,
the parlors, palaces of ardor and cash.
They live as in an ant farm
built of frosted glass.
You can see them mating
with the wife-body machines,
the cash flow of each courtship,
which might go on flowing
and ebbing for days, until

a senior male relative or friend
drags the addict home.

In my favorite video blackjack game,
two disembodied, white-gloved hands
shoot their cuffs,
snap and flex the deck
with slight impatience: *Your bet?*
The chip-clink's ultrarealistic
on the cyberfelt, dollar a bet.
Phantom Belle, that's my machine.

SOUL IN SPACE

How did it come to be
that a particular human loneliness
set forth into clouds of ignorance
so as to more closely examine itself?
Why one and so few others?

I stand among shoulder-high canes,
looking directly into their barbed
inner dark to the snake, or caterpillar—
actually a handful of blackberries
in the green shade, reptilian
yet warm, momentarily still.

I want my obituary to say that
I wrote in the language of dogs
and not that I sat sprinkling
black letters on a white ladder,
leading my own eye down
one rung at a time
until the dog was gone.

NECK EXERCISES

Because I have arthritis in three
vertebrae, I do yoga and lift
small weights. Strange,
what the exercises dislodge:
a Popeye cartoon,
pirates and skeletons—
what's so indelible about that?
Or the way a dog's eye looked
in a painting, how it followed me.
I like the spinal rotations,
the flex in the tree of history,
part green, part stiffened by bark.
It sprouts a shoot of memory,
a line I once abandoned:
all their hope in their shoulder blades—
it came from seeing some fifteen-
or sixteen-year-old girls on a summer dock—
why should that survive? I guess
it's why I'm standing here before you,
pumping the tiny barbells.

TWO GREEDS

I'm greedy for my intelligent
little cat, old Miami,
who's taught me to speak
a bit of her tongue.
Spine a string of gray beads,
she's stalking a savanna
of high grass, her mouth
slightly open, enhancing
her powers of smell.
I think she hunts the memory
of what it was like to see.

On the other hand,
I chafe to begin building
her cage, the poem.
Every moment forks:
right to love, left to work.
The second greed is for worship,
for grief and joy made permanent
in words. Poetry's a temple for one.
One human being, one god.

INFANT PEARLS

On the subjects of poetry and love,
I ask a lot of questions that are
the children of the questions
I should be asking,
but S just dances out there
with her new escort,
in her string of infant pearls
and a black bra showing
through white eyelet.
I want to be just like her,
half bride, half widow,
going to God in my mind.

DRUG-TAKING

When I talked to Mom,
I could hear her drinking,
sip-pauses like a smoker's,
the meniscus of her voice
about to break with news,
crocus splitting the dirt,
first to tell.

Diagnosis: depression.
Self-medication.
Early evening, second glass;
maybe she could hear me
hitting on a joint, blowing
away from the receiver,
and heard it as a sigh.

MAH-JONGG

Grandma kept her mah-jongg
in a little casket—
tiny hinges, shallow drawerfuls
of bamboo and ivory tiles.
A game too hard for kids;
not a toy; hands off.

The object is to dismantle
a city of tiny headstones,
each carved with bird, flower,
or character denoting one
of the four winds, seasons, dragons,
et cetera, or one of the many suits.
Mah is the sound of flax in wind;
jongg means "sparrow chatter."
Birdsong and flaxsong,
the sound of the tiles—
tusk and bamboo,
the clattering to life
of winds and dragons.
There's danger of addiction
in the sound of flax in wind,
in sparrow music. I bought a set
on eBay so I could hear it too.

TECH HELP

My bonsai teacher says to *quit doing it like a girl.*
I'm pruning the root-ball of a *Podocarpus,*
or Buddhist pine, trained semicascade.

The first time Dad fell,
the femur broke in eleven places
due to his artificial knee (titanium and steel).
A rod screwed to the bones in thirteen places
didn't work, and the graft stayed weak.
For two years he fought his wheelchair
into near submission. The grand finale
was him riding it down two flights of stairs
without tipping over or falling out.
The nurses loved him.

The last time I called tech help
I got George in Salt Lake, at work
at six in the morning their time.
He was very helpful.
I offered to write a note for his file,
but he said, *It's OK, Chase.*
Your compliment is enough.

THE QUALITY OF STRIVING

Eye-catching as a dog on a chain,
tough muscled, brash,
talking fifty-fifty words/harmonica,
Bob Dylan let himself as an old man
sit in on the songs.
I want words half zendo,
half casino like his,
cruder and more fluent than this,
with a swelling inevitability about them,
an itch, the way a bud must itch
before it breaks.

If you think northern spring
is more beautiful than spring in the South,
then on some level you understand
that I write by the light of the secret
Protestant pride in asceticism,
the most seductive Buddha of all.

My war pits sleep's enthrallments
against those of consciousness.
I often encounter a miniature,
localized tiredness,
droopy yellow flag marking
a tree to come down.
Next second I'm setting out to master
the subspecies of all conifers in the region
and the first five hundred
Latin vocabulary flash cards.

It's late again and I'm tired,
too tired to take up the great
work of introspection,

to be a spur to myself.
But what drives me
to be a spur?
Why not a lullaby sung
in the hammock's hinge-screak,
sound of the word *squander?*
What hungry ghost in me
rises and strips off
the self-scented sheets before dawn?

RAIN IN IVY

I'm pondering the question,
What hunts the leaf? No answer.
In the monastery kitchen,
a dozen of us work in silence.
A koan is a monastery in your own head,
said Ta-hui, and as I set out to peel
a crate of acorn squash, I think he's right.
Rain makes the ivy move, as if
it were actively climbing.
It's metaphor to which my mind clings,
always too busy to see its own true nature.
I sharpen the knives just as my father
taught me, except here you don't spit
to wet the stone. I found the pocketknife
he lost, and hid it. I still have it.
I'm wondering where it is,
so when the drum sounds
marking the end of work time
I still don't know what hunts the leaf.

THINNING SHADOW OF MIAMI

Hindquarters locked by arthritis,
Miami's thinning shadow
scrambles up the back of my chair
using only her arms
and turns to a little fur stole
on my shoulders, opening and closing
the clasps of her beautiful claws.
I was typing, and now I'm weeping
tears so pure and streaming
I don't recognize them as my own.
Soon I'll feel only a draft in her place,
but that's true of everything I love.
These tears must come from a well
I didn't know was there.

DRESS REHEARSAL

The dress rehearsal is not going well.
The actor playing Grief
is quite drunk and refuses
to follow the script.
She's turning the whole show
into a public confession
with herself recast as the star.
It's Guilt's part she wants.

Bodo lay in his thin fur,
his ribs on the ribs of the vent,
watching the slow traffic of the house.
I berate myself for having paid
you such poor attention
those days of your dying,
my brown-striped boy.
I'm sorry you died at the vet's
with a needle in your shaved skinny arm.
I'm sorry, Bodo.

THE CEILING

I'm conscious of my bones
where they touch the porcelain.
The tub stays cold beneath
the water's heat,
so it's the two colds that
recognize each other here
in this grotto of earthly delights,
candles enlivening
the tile overhead,
the perfumed foam
I lie beneath.

A word alighting
on the tongue-tip,
then gone again. . . .
And my eyes are changing.
Oh, the fussing over glasses.
The mind sees its own machines
blacken and break down,
beaten back into the earth
near the railroad bed:
wire carts, sodden nests
beneath the overpass.
Who sleeps there,
among the dead umbrellas?

Uh-oh, I'm lying here glistening
and warm in the river Styx
thinking of death again,
bones in a catacomb.
A trickle keeps it hot,
but the suds are gone.
Look at my fifty-two-year-old legs,
starting to ache
for their last lover, the dirt.

NEW ENGLAND SLATE PANE

Mom has already made arrangements
for a spot inside the churchyard wall
among the old Yankee slates,
some fallen, and the granites
from foreign places,
tilted by frost.
A mason sets them straight
again each spring.
Perennials for the formal beds
accepted with gratitude;
no other plantings allowed.
Cut flowers may be laid on the graves.
Someone might leave
plastic tulips as a joke.
Otherwise, silence, nothing,
trees living their interior lives,
visitors wandering
among the oldest stones.
This is where she wants to lie,
next to wind-pruned beach roses,
paths of crushed shells.

Somebody finally bought that farm
and orchard I like to drive past
at blossom time,
mud runnels in the roads,
trees way past mature.
For ten years no one's come
to prune or feed or mow the aisles.
Bare scatterings of flowers
alight on broken branches.
Who let it all go?
What broke in the family?

Now the elderly apples will spend
their twilight in the paintings of a man
who bought them
in order to study their end.
She wants her marker spare like that,
just name and dates.
Time's black-and-white bouquet.

CITIES OF MIND

From up here on the parapets
I can see skeletons of meaning strewn
among stones, all the way east
to childhood's shaded rooms.
To the west lie the cities
I've not yet imagined,
and those I never will.

Let's admit it's an addiction,
this scribbling-turned-typing.
How else might we speak of it?
As an anxiety? In any case,
I seem to like its fangs in my heart.

On Dad's eightieth birthday
we had a little party
in the living room,
the whole herd of wheelchairs
drawn like magnets to the smell of cake,
the snuffed-out candles.

I'm sorry my father keeps barging in here.
He usually doesn't stay very long.
He's an old man who was once a man.
And one of Mom's shadows falls
from time to time, just so you know.

Jim Richardson says, "All work
is the avoidance of harder work"—
true in my case. When the carpenters
started on the porch, I moved
the computer to the guest room,
where I had to crawl under the bed

66

with an extension cord to get juice.
Then I had to fight hedges
of castoffs, wrapping papers and ribbons,
a plastic serpent's nest of
strapping tape unwilling
to stay in the wastebasket,
the snake's name something like
anaconda, boa constrictor, python,
rattler... oh, I know: *time consumer.*

Confetti, glitter, glamour,
the frosting flowers and the hopeless
little figurines glued to the cake—
what happens to those?
Do people save them?
Pass them down the generations?

When Nan got into coyote bait,
I drove her through the wee hours
to the fancy animal hospital far away,
thinking, *Let her live, let her not suffer,*
then, *Let her die quickly,*
thus killing the snake of my fear
along with the dog.

See what happens if you leave
the blossoms on the tree?
They go on blooming,
obscuring the thorns,
and before you know it
a scarf of identity has distracted you,
a jewel of history glinted in your eye. . . .

Raised on the classic myths,
I see the drift nets of latitude

and longitude on the night sky
inhabited by beasts and gods.
On Pegasus I fled the hunter,
the centaur, the satyr,
riding the star-horse out to free
the great and lesser bears,
the major and minor dogs,
caged in their constellations.

THE PACK

A sleek black tail lies across
the page as I write.
Everyone's here this afternoon,
Kili's head on my lap, double-weighted
with her boredom,
Miami riffling and ruffling a catalog,
Nan standing by with her ball.
Sometimes I see Bodo's ghost
in the hall. Is a ghost a wish?
A squirt of neurochemicals
making it almost possible
to see my brown Bodo boy,
but not quite?

Miami always did look like an owl,
ring-necked and with a feathery delicacy
to her fur, as if she could be plucked.
Now that she's old she seems to be
collapsing by minuscule degrees
into a bird skeleton
snoozing in her sweater nest,
pin-claws clasping
if she's feeling uncaressed,
under the seventy-five-watt sun.

The dogs know fifty human words,
at least, including abstractions
like Boring Time and Kili's favorite game,
Laser Safari, its name a struck match!
Glazed with dog endorphins,
her eyes track the maddening
ruby rodent-dot into a shoe.
Watch out it might dart out and go right up your leg!

Heart attack! Heart attack laser!
Or hide in the sofa cushions!
Mountain goat! Mountain goat laser!

Nan's six distinct barks
say all she has to say.
She makes herself perfectly clear,
playing up and down
the scale of her anxiety.
Poor skinny Nan,
whelped in her first year,
my lean shivery divorce dog,
all bones and rigging,
pink bellied,
hurling herself into her task.
What is her task? And what now?
To be without a task—
that's Nan's anxiety and reason for being,
soft feathered, wanton for love,
only just beginning to trust that she's
a permanent member of the pack.

OK. It's Boring Time. No more ball.
Come lie down. No more ball.

Bodo in the corner of my eye,
not in my lap.
No more splitting the can
between two cats.

Nan's tongue relishes a bone.
No one takes Nan's bone,
not even Kili, Opus One,
the dominant dog.

After scolding, the dogs go silent and watch
the UPS truck from the guest room window,
letting out an occasional rude *woof*.

THE TAIL

A tiny muscle
slackened in my eyelid.
I felt its weight,
though in the mirror
nothing showed.
Now it remembers
itself to me, nerve
flickering as if to say,
Wake up! This might
be the pinnacle dusk!
Study the hardwoods
turning to bone in the snow!

Stay with me, dogs,
black-and-white spirits
asleep by the door,
none of us yet wandering among
the hordes that Dante saw.
We're all of us studying how
napkin gets demoted to dust rag,
towel to dog towel.
I put my hand on Nan's
spotted belly and smooth
the coarse feathers of her tail.
She sighs when I leave her.
Come, Nan.
Come lie beside my chair
and be my muse.

4. HAIL AND FAREWELL

THE MYTHS

Italy and Greece lay in ruins,
inhabited by beasts: the Minotaur
in his labyrinth, the *scrush* of his hide
against its walls; the blinded Cyclops
groping for Ulysses among the sheep.
Dad taught us all the myths.

Up on Mount Olympus
people disguised themselves
as animals. It was like that then.
It's not like that now.
Back then you were half animal
if your father was a god.

CINDERBLOCK

On the first warm day,
the aides fret about his pate,
fetch his hat. I push him
out the automatic doors
into the pallid sun.
Dad thinks we should
stay put until all the Indians
are back in their tepees,
but right now he's off to teach
a Latin class. Where are his keys?
They're a few miles away,
in the past, where he's no longer
active in the community.
I steer him along the asphalt paths
of the grounds: bark mulch,
first green shoots,
puddle of coffee by a car.
I loop around so he can discover
the pile of construction materials twice,
the word *cinderblock* coming to him
more quickly the second time.

JOYRIDE

Two aides get Dad into the car
on the second try.
He meddles with his seat belt,
pats the dash, rubs his hands
as if putting on lotion.
The old farms excite him,
so I drive out past
dazed herds of condos
to where big tractors
are spreading manure,
moving hay.
Past his eyes drift
cows hock-deep in mud,
a man scraping a house,
all of it passing
at thirty miles an hour,
alpacas and merino sheep
prized for their wool,
ruined silo,
bird dog crossing the road,
woman looking up
from planting a tree.
I say I once drove past
a field of camels in Vermont.
He starts to tell a similar story
but none comes to mind.

When we were kids he'd fishtail
up the twisty road to East Rock Park,
throwing gravel, making crash sounds,
heading straight for the tree.
At the top: a monument
to war dead, disgraced by graffiti.

At night, teenagers parked
their cars by the stone tower
(he never said why).
Someone had drawn a penis
on the plaque of names,
the war dead who lay
inside the monument,
in their graves.

The same aides stand by,
but Dad won't get out of the car.
He's headed back to his childhood,
which lives on in a few souls,
his daughters,
but they come only once a week,
and no one else knows the way.
When they muscle him
back into the wheelchair,
he stabs with weak elbows,
canine yelp.
The doors open inward
toward the aquarium,
clear tubes forcing bubbles
from a ship wrecked on lurid gravel.
He likes to park close to the
pump-and-filter's white noise.
I tell him I'll see him next week.
He says, *Give me ten minutes to pack.*

OLIVETTI

Dad has four typewriters,
each beaten into silence:
two Olympia manuals, circa 1970,
an early Brother electric,
and a used IBM Selectric
of which he never quite got the hang.
It was petty and argumentative,
erasing the wrong mistake,
cussing him with kkkkk's.
He used to have another,
an old Olivetti with a green
case like a turtle shell
and a lock with a little key.
Platen spattered with Wite-Out,
it typed smudgy crooked letters
with oddball accents
and no dollar sign.
On this machine I wrote
my first words to the world.
He gave it to the aide who
reads to him, for her kid.

ANIMAL CAUTION

Whenever I touch the cairn
marking the summit
of one of my parents,
touch the top stone,
an animal caution comes over me,
sinew and muscle like the brook's,
a sudden shivering
green-brown flame.
Soon they will be constellations,
and I a small tower of stones.

VERIZON

My father had been "climbing,"
so they moved him down
toward the nurses' station;
very confusing: first a new room
and now his telephone is dead.
He repeats the word *Verizon*
at the speed of a slow hammock
while I call Repair on my cell.
This is not how it's meant to be,
the wire serpent recoiling
from him as if to strike
at his memory, his recovery,
lithe black spiral,
strong willed, heavy dial tone
swinging upside down. Sometimes
when he pushes the luminous buttons
a woman tells him all about Verizon,
using the word in many beautiful sentences,
spreading it out for him like a golf course
on which he looks forward to playing,
but sometimes he answers her rudely,
manhandling the receiver,
cursing Verizon and his outlaw hands.
Or he's pissed because the aide
brings him the telephone, saying,
It's your daughter isn't that nice?
as if it were any business of hers.
You couldn't film this. No one
would be able to bear it,
skeletons everywhere,
riding around on silver wheels,
pure oxygen piped straight to skulls

crowned by near-colorless
chains of proteins, the hair.
I saw not just my father's
long bones but also the knowledge
they withhold from him,
catheter, sponge bath,
titanium and steel.
Oh hell, the tea's cold.
Verizon, izon, izon, zon.
Birds of cyberspace sing in his ear,
bright notes and numbers, urging him
to *Visit our Web site to find out more.*

MY LISTENER

When hope forms a bud of prayer,
who picks it?
Words in all languages
yearn toward the stars,
confessing and beseeching.

I talk to a masculine higher power
half god, half human.
When he sits calm and golden,
spine straight as the Buddha's,
my own spine yearns upward
toward the clean sky of his face.
But when he lounges
on the butcher's throne,
setting wars on fire from afar
then hunting in the gutted,
rotting lands, he's my enemy, the one
who lifted my father from the cradle
in his claws so many years ago,
then let him fall,
a stick of driftwood someone saved,
provenance unknown.

Dad waits for cocktail hour,
cookies and juice,
repeating the words *voice mail* to himself,
anxious about the new technologies,
the fax and the microwave.
At night in his stainless crib
he addresses
the One Who Knows Everything
Yet Does Nothing, who ekes out
a bright fistful of candies

to keep the game alive
while the child prays for death,
shaking the safety rails.

When my Listener shows me his ribs,
all my austerities gather around me,
earnest and gray, and I vow
to make myself invisible,
possessionless,
a servant of the world.
But he's only a demigod,
and jealous. He commands me
to meet him in private.
I tell him the truth insofar
as I know it. He says nothing.
We always meet in private.
When he whips his starving flocks
I'm there alone with him.

SLING

The meanest thing my father ever said,
he said to my cousin, who told me:
She'll make the world's worst wife.
Thank you, cousin, for tearing away
one of my veils.

When Mom came to see us
I fell from the tree house, and had to lug
a pail of stones around all summer
because the elbow healed slightly bent.
That straightened the arm.

Oh, when does childhood end?
In the globe of the night sky
the inner stars are falling.
I leave him in a room like a baby's
but without toys.

LET'S TALK

Let's talk about his death,
right now in progress,
and about the BBs
the angry child put in his milk,
her silence as he swallowed them.
Now she remembers it
and he has no memory,
so it's her possession now.
She can give it away or use it all up.
She has not yet finished using it.

DON'T WASTE THAT FUEL

Dad says everything was fine
until I threw a wrench into the fire.
And no, he does not want
help turning the goddamned
wheelchair around.

Eliza shows him where Portugal is
on the map. France, Italy, Greece.
Dad wants her to point out
the Saint Katharine Line. What's that?
It's the line between "Thou shalt have dogs"
and "Thou shalt not have dogs."

Paper cup of juice, banana.
While the aide thickens Dad's juice
for ease of swallowing, he says,
You're a good-looking woman.
Don't waste that fuel on a lawn mower.

THE SOUP

I went to see Dad at the home.
The soup was turkey corn chowder
with wild rice. Not bad, considering
we ate it in the waiting room
of the house of Death.

EMPTY CRADLE SONGS

I think about the rooms
in which my parents slept
as children, what hung
on the walls. In Mom's room,
angels with watering cans
sprinkled the green and blooming
earth and all its creatures,
still there at night
under the see-in-the-dark stars.
Angel rain fell on her infant fear
of the furnace-clank,
her breath pumped from small
moist bellows into the night
air of the room in which she slept
right up to the wedding,
the getaway.

Dad's room was erased when he
went off to school at fourteen.
By Christmas it was a guest room.
New wax, new blinds.
He remembers the gray-green
lawns of the interior,
many clocks ticking,
but not his room.
Not a trace of it,
though he remembers his toys.
There's a picture of him
with a little wheelbarrow,
probably two years old,
wailing, making baby fists,
yet picked up by no one,
not even whoever's standing
ten feet away from him
snapping the shot.

SEXY FORENSICS

Because his mind is dying,
he sees not the lovers' lane
of wheelchairs in the dayroom,
linked by held hands,
but the long hall at night,
men and women lying
behind closed doors,
some lying together,
others alone as in a morgue,
where a light blinks
outside his room if he stirs,
and women come quickly
when he coughs up
something that stinks.

DEATH'S PORTRAIT

I just caught myself in the mirror
with a look like one of my father's,
a forward-leaning absorption,
greedy, thinking of itself.
I saw him animated in me,
jaw set with glee and slyness,
his future ghost dropping in
to remind me he'll always
be with me, even when I no longer
know where or who I am.

I rented a boat and went
fishing in the Caribbean.
The guy who took me was
proud of his sonar,
acres of ocean on a little screen.
A black shape might be a big fish,
might be a school of smalls.
We rode around all morning
watching the screen.
There was nothing there.

REMOTE OUTPOSTS

A buck just coming into spike
stopped at the wood's edge.
We regarded each other,
me taking a step back,
putting down the trowel,
making no eye contact,
him flaring at the smell of me,
tossing his head, then curious,
emboldened, stepping forward.
Our eyes took each other in,
the way in a mirror a finger
can never touch itself.

Because Dad watched *Maverick*
with me a few times,
it was as if we'd been there together
in the Wild West, him the tall, dark stranger
and me the sidekick, orphan, runaway
learning to play cards in the saloons.
We slept by a campfire under the stars.
Once we saw two hundred horses elope
through broken fence to the high pastures,
the very edge of grass.
He said, *Come on, kid.*
Let's saddle up and hit the dusty trail.

DOG BISCUITS

After my father's cremation,
my sisters and I agreed
to bury him privately
when the ground thawed.
One will plant a flowering tree,
one see to the stone and its cutting,
one call the grave digger and the town clerk.
It'll be just us, the daughters,
presiding over ashes that could be
any mammal's, or those of any love
dispersible by wind.

Let's bury the secret violence to his dogs,
Pompey and Tara, Juba and Molly,
their ashes already gone to this ground.
And his "escapades," as Mom called them.
Here withers that branch of the tree.

Let's bury the ring inscribed
In perpetuum ave atque vale (translated
"Hail and farewell" by my father,
"Hello, and good-bye forever" by Mom,
a token dating back to the First Separation)
and a tennis ball for canine shades.
Your dad is with his dogs now,
said more than one person at the funeral.

It'll be just us, the three inheritors,
on a raw windy day in Death's kingdom,
lifting our eyes from the hole
to the mountains hazed with spring,
saying, *In perpetuum ave atque vale,*
minor god of our father.
Let's each of us drop a few
dog biscuits into his grave.

THE RANGE

The cemetery has one of the two
best views in town (the other being
from the dump), built on the same
high, rocky land, the idea being
that beauty belongs to everyone.
It's why Dad called the cemetery
"the other landfill."

From up here you can see
most of the Range:
Wolf Jaws, Armstrong, Gothics, Saddleback, Basin,
and a stretch of the Ausable in late thaw,
ice breaking up, shards cast off and remarried,
the river flinching, flexing, isometric,
a granite beauty to which it is impossible
to be unfaithful. He loved it as I do,
above all other loves.

5. THE PLAIN PICTURE

VESTIBULE

What etiquette holds us back
from more intimate speech,
especially now, at the end of the world?
Can't we begin a conversation
here in the vestibule,
then gradually move it inside?
What holds us back
from saying things outright?
We've killed the earth.
Yet we speak of other things.
Our words should cauterize
all wounds to the truth.

A NEGATIVE OF SNOW

Ice on the puddles,
in the cups of fallen leaves.
I'd walk with Dad and a handful
of other men, the setters working
the fields, the underbrush.
It was my job to carry the birds.
I'd have them all plucked
by the time we got back to the car.
On the walk out I'd look
for puddles I'd missed
and break them.

Though many moonless nights
have fallen on the grave
like a negative of snow,
Dad's wheelchair sometimes
flashes in my mind, and I hear
the bleating down the hall,
a voice berating its god,
his worthless anodynes,
and the doctors who were
at that very moment
increasing his morphine,
having failed to note
the word *alcoholic* on his chart,
meaning that his damaged liver
routed the opiates straight
to his brain, his beautiful fragile brain,
which I had not yet finished loving.
My father, who still had manners,
who was a hardwood, a tough tree.
That was his first death.

IMMEDIATE REVISION

I love milkweed, especially
summer's taut linen pods
just splitting, reluctant to part
with the white silk, the seeds.
And then the bits of cirrus
snagged in the field.

The sky I'm trying to paint
changes fast, keeps fooling me,
slurring the intermarriages of clouds,
hemorrhaging darkness and chill,
banking the fire on Pitchoff's rocky spine.
My painting ends up a night sky,
so I add a couple of constellations,
sketching in the star-beasts.

Such carnage of ferns,
clanging and male shouts
from the work site—
they're dredging coal tar
from the brook. Big machines
root around in the woods.
But in moonlight the toxic trees
look heaped with snow,
so profuse are their flowers.

NEWS OF THE WAR

The whole family lay out on blankets
to see *Sputnik*, 1957. Chilly evening.
Balsam in the wind. We all saw it:
the first fake light in the heavens.

On CNN they're interviewing coaches,
calling the plays on large maps,
pointing out the flash of sun
on armor, reptilian tanks
flexing in the world of sand,
carving a new road.

All the inscrutable clouds of my childhood
have come back to see me.
They're my escorts.
One of them takes me to a room
at Motel 8 with a picture of Canada geese
called *Heading South.*
The sky's an unreal blue, and the birds' eyes
glow as if they were imagining a lake
the painter never touched.

Some asshole called, wanting to buy Dad's car
the last week of his driving in the world.
He'd heard from Gibb's cousin
we wanted five thousand dollars.
I told him he'd heard wrong.
It was a two-year-old Subaru Forester
with twelve thousand miles on it.
He pissed me off.

THE HOUR OF THE BISCUIT

The children's shrink wrote in a notebook
swollen with papers, drawings—
friendly, because you could see
she talked to lots of kids like you
and wrote their stories in her book.
Kind Dr. C, with her naked
girl and boy dolls.

Dog barks; human opens door.
It's time for the evening news,
for the pack to gather by the TV.
A scotch, a glass of wine, the mail.
Then dogs sit while humans hide
many tiny treats throughout the room.
The Hour of the Biscuit is upon us.

What does it mean,
"to let something go"?
It sounds like releasing a trout
or a bird with a healed wing,
but they can't fly or swim
back to the life before.
Letting go is forgetting.
I know; I didn't want to believe it, either.
But memory dies when it
lies down deep in the forest,
leaving no trail of crumbs.

MONASTERY NIGHTS

I like to think about the monastery
as I'm falling asleep, so that it comes
and goes in my mind like a screen saver.
I conjure the lake of the zendo,
rows of dark boats still unless
someone coughs or otherwise
ripples the calm.
I can hear the four AM slipperiness
of sleeping bags as people turn over
in their bunks. The ancient bells.

When I was first falling in love with Zen,
I burned incense called *Kyonishiki,*
"Kyoto Autumn Leaves,"
made by the Shoyeido Incense Company,
Kyoto, Japan. To me it smelled like
earnestness and ether, and I tried to imagine
a consciousness ignorant of me.
I just now lit a stick of it. I had to run downstairs
for some rice to hold it upright in its bowl,
which had been empty for a while,
a raku bowl with two fingerprints
in the clay. It calls up the monastery gate,
the massive door demanding I recommit myself
in the moments of both its opening
and its closing, its weight now mine.
I wanted to know what I was,
and thought I could find the truth
where the floor hurts the knee.

I understand no one I consider to be religious.
I have no idea what's meant when someone says
they've been intimate with a higher power.

I seem to have been born without a god receptor.
I have fervor but seem to lack
even the basic instincts of the many seekers,
mostly men, I knew in the monastery,
sitting zazen all night,
wearing their robes to near-rags
boy-stitched back together with unmatched thread,
smoothed over their laps and tucked under,
unmoving in the long silence,
the field of grain ripening, heavy tasseled,
field of sentient beings turned toward candles,
flowers, the Buddha gleaming
like a vivid little sports car from his niche.

What is the mind that precedes
any sense we could possibly have
of ourselves, the mind of self-ignorance?
I thought that the divestiture of self
could be likened to the divestiture
of words, but I was wrong.
It's not the same work.
One's a transparency
and one's an emptiness.

Kyonishiki. . . .
Today I'm painting what Mom
calls no-colors, grays and browns,
evergreens: what's left of the woods
when autumn's come and gone.
And though he died, Dad's here,
still forgetting he's no longer
married to Annie,
that his own mother is dead,
that he no longer owns a car.
I told them not to make any trouble
or I'd send them both home.

Surprise half inch of snow.
What good are words?

And what about birches in moonlight,
Russell handing me the year's
first chanterelle—
Shouldn't God feel like that?

I aspire to "a self-forgetful,
perfectly useless concentration,"
as Elizabeth Bishop put it.
So who shall I say I am?
I'm a prism, an expressive temporary
sentience, a pinecone falling.
I can hear my teacher saying, *No.*
That misses it.
Buddha goes on sitting through the century,
leaving me alone in the front hall,
which has just been cleaned and smells of pine.

WORK LIBIDO

The year I turned fourteen,
Grandma taught me five-card stud
and took my allowance for the week.
In casinos I usually play blackjack.
I like the speed and scale,
companion strangers fingering their chips,
and the background ruckus of slots
and cybersounds, coins
cascading into man-sized Dixie cups.

Each sentience is brief, is it not?
Therefore I'm trying to record whatever
I can of the instantly squandered present
so I can say in stone-plain words
what sentience is.

Rules: Tell the truth. No decoration. Remember death.

As far as I can tell, there's no
such thing as a "present moment."
To me they're like atoms:
faster than imagination,
intermarried, unto themselves,
their boundaries invisible
and their numbers unknown.
I think of them as paint rather
than as words, though of course
the two smear where they overlap.

Gamblers and poets share
a passion for what's next: the flush
disguised as a boat with a hole
(that's poker talk), or a rift

in the poem, a soft spot that yields
the sticky perfume of pine pitch,
like burned honey but resinous,
spicy, antiseptic, a conduit straight
to childhood with its ferns
incompletely unfurled,
their not-quite-mature spores
glistening like caviar among green feathers.
And to the little diamond snake that slithered
round my neck (but only for while).

Sorry, I'm quite distracted.
A breeze from the next poem
has slipped into this one,
so my mind is playing with
the sound of reptilian fountains
and the racing colors of the chips,
the clay and composite resins
always cool to the touch.
The playground is empty,
and from here the casino sounds
like an ocean of tiny bells.

THE INSECTS OF SEPTEMBER

One of the middle-aged carpenters
working on the porch is teaching
a younger one, an apprentice,
by explaining exactly what it is
he's doing. That's all. The kid
picks it up fast by following,
and they hardly talk, each off
in his own mid-afternoon dream,
except for every once in a while
the older guy says, *Complete attention!*
when he's about to demonstrate
something important.

Never have I seen such a green
gauze of wings over the field—
the insects of September
entering the beforelife
just as the afterlife begins.

Chickenhearted, that's what I am,
quivering and fluffing in the dust,
making minor linguistic disturbances,
my eye already fixed
on the next bit of gold grain,
and the next, among the gravel.
Still, I will go on loving
and losing the world until I die.
I want to be awake when the synapses
flicker and fail, and memory simplifies the past.

THOUGHT SATELLITE

What a strange world this is,
dime-sized Earth in the background
of Death's portrait in the dining room.
It spins on, its nations charred,
its altars still on fire,
its playgrounds still.

I think of poems as a series
of small harsh rebirths—
I keep passing myself in the halls
of a house where every room
has a second door,
so I never have to go out
the way I came in.

It's quitting time. The carpenters
working on the porch left at four,
and the dogs need a run.
So good-bye; I'm dying out
of this communion now,
into the next rebirth:
an August afternoon at the pinnacle,
scent of balsam spiked by rain,
the field glittering.

Somebody's chain saw
barks at the afternoon.

Andy Gates is flying
his Cessna all over the valley,
looking for his girlfriend's car.

Well, that's it. See you.

NOTES ON THE TEXT

"Skeleton": The Bob Dylan quote is from *Don't Look Back*, D. A. Pennebaker's documentary of Dylan's 1965 tour of England.

"Dangerous Playgrounds": The quoted passage is misremembered from "The Mystic," by Cale Young Rice (*The Little Book of Modern Verse*, Houghton Mifflin, 1917). The poem also paraphrases parts of *The Tale of Two Bad Mice*, by Beatrix Potter (F. Warne, 1904).

"Tutelage": The quoted hymn is "Fairest Lord Jesus," written by seventeenth-century German Jesuits; "When the student is ready, the teacher appears" is a Zen aphorism.

"Cities of Mind": The James Richardson quote is from *Vectors: Aphorisms & Ten-Second Essays* (Ausable Press, 2001).

ABOUT THE AUTHOR

Chase Twichell has published five previous books of poetry:
The Snow Watcher, The Ghost of Eden, Perdido, The Odds, and *Northern
Spy.* She is also the translator, with Tony K. Stewart, of *The Lover
of God* by Rabindranath Tagore (Copper Canyon), and co-editor
of *The Practice of Poetry: Writing Exercises from Poets Who Teach.* Her
work has received fellowships from the National Endowment
for the Arts, the Artists Foundation, the New Jersey State
Council on the Arts, and the John Simon Guggenheim
Memorial Foundation, and a Literature Award from the
American Academy of Arts and Letters. In 1997 she won the
Alice Fay Di Castagnola Award from the Poetry Society of
America for *The Snow Watcher.* She was awarded a Smart Family
Foundation Award in 2004 for poems published in the *Yale
Review.* After teaching for many years—Warren Wilson College,
The University of Alabama, Goddard College, Hampshire
College, and Princeton University (1990–1999)—she left
academia to start Ausable Press, which publishes contemporary
poetry. She lives in Upstate New York with her husband, the
novelist Russell Banks.

The Chinese character for poetry is made up of two parts: "word" and "temple." It also serves as pressmark for Copper Canyon Press.

Founded in 1972, Copper Canyon Press remains dedicated to publishing poetry exclusively, from Nobel laureates to new and emerging authors. The Press thrives with the generous patronage of readers, writers, book-sellers, librarians, teachers, students, and funders—everyone who shares the conviction that poetry invigorates the language and sharpens our appreciation of the world.

Major funding has been provided by:

The Paul G. Allen Family Foundation
Lannan Foundation
National Endowment for the Arts
Washington State Arts Commission

For information and catalogs:

COPPER CANYON PRESS
Post Office Box 271
Port Townsend, Washington 98368
360-385-4925
www.coppercanyonpress.org

This book was designed by Phil Kovacevich and typeset in Centaur.

The roman capitals of Centaur were designed as a titling font by Bruce Rogers for the Metropolitan Museum of Art, New York, 1912–14. Subsequently lowercase letters were added, and the typeface was released by Monotype in 1929. The italic (called Arrighi) was designed by Frederic Warde in 1925, and based on Ludovico Arrighi's chancery typeface, Venice, designed in 1520. The typeface is named after the publication it was first used in, Maurice de Guérin's *The Centaur*.